Treasures in Heaven

Discover The Life Changing Nuggets In God's Word

by Katherine E. Gardner

Treasures in Heaven

Discover The Life Changing Nuggets In God's Word

by Katherine E. Gardner

Graphic Design by:
Simpson Communications * 248.443.9880
simpsoncommunications@comcast.net

Treasures in Heaven
Discover the Life-changing Nuggets in God's Word
ISBN 0-9724116-0-7
Copyright © 2003 by Katherine E. Gardner

Published by *Treasures in Heaven, Inc.*
51690 Hale Lane
Chesterfield Twp, MI 48051
To order more copies of this book,
please call 866-308-6235, Ext. 20

Printed in the United States of America. All rights reserved under International Copyright Law. Contents and/or cover may not be reproduced in whole or in part in any form without the express written consent of the publisher.

Dedication

To Sylvia,
My mentor, cheerleader, and friend.

Treasures in Heaven

Foreword

Words are like seeds. They have creative power. Words are the way we give life to our faith. Words are the substance of what we hope for. We can frame our desires, as well as secure the will of God for our lives by the power of the spoken Word. I have done what Katherine is encouraging you to do through the pages of this book. Particularly, as an unmarried woman, filled with a desire for marriage and family, I was challenged to believe God in this area of my life. After all, why do we have to believe God for a husband? It was easy to profess His Word for salvation, forgiveness, healing, or financial provisions, but did I need to do that for a man?

After seeing consistent manifestations of God's power in other areas of my life, as well as answered prayer for others, and after passively waiting 10 years for something to happen in this area, I became aggressive in my faith and was totally convinced that I could have what I say! Emphatically, I say, *yes*! *Every wise woman builds her house (Proverbs 14:1).* Day-by-day, for two years, the Lord taught me wisdom and filled my heart and mouth with faith-filled words from the Scriptures, not for "just a man," but for a husband more rare and precious, who would love me the way Christ loves His Church.

I am a witness and can testify that far too many believers are silent. My silence has been broken! My fiance and I look forward to exchanging our vows and continuing to build our marriage on the word of faith! Friend, you can prophesy your future. In *Section Four* of this book, you will find a model prayer for a mate, which is a reflection of what I did, and a practical guide for getting aggressive in your faith. **Go for it!**

Treasures in Heaven

May Katherine's work encourage your heart and make it easier for you to speak the Word of God.

Delightfully in His Service,

Lois E. Vaughn

Minister Stancel was married to Mr. Nathaniel Vaughn in 2003, after this writing.

Preface

Treasures in Heaven is simple enough for the enjoyment of those who are new in the things of God, yet rich enough to be used as an effective learning and teaching tool for the most spiritually advanced. There is something for every reader:

- Excellent source of information and Scripture concerning Holy Spirit

- Healing Scriptures and confessions for the sick, the health-conscious, or the uninformed

- Comforting Scriptures for those fearful concerning recent national and world events

- Those who value and seek after wisdom will benefit from the Proverbs confessions.

- Those who are seeking spiritual and moral excellence will benefit from the Colossians and Philippians confessions.

- Model prayers exhibit how to pray according to the Scriptures.

Treasures in Heaven

- Phenomenal insight as to how one personally confesses the Word of God

Treasures in Heaven is also excellent material for outreach programs and churches that include:

- College campuses
- Prisons, jails, and halfway houses
- Hospitals (visitation ministry or chaplain material)
- Youth groups and homes

Churches that are teaching their congregations about the power of the spoken Word of God are exploding all around the globe. I'm reminded of the world's largest and fastest growing church, *Yoido Full Gospel Church* in Seoul Korea. There, Dr. Yonggi Cho, Pastor, teaches his congregation of over 700,000 members the power and simplicity of the "Words of Life" found in the Bible.

Acknowledgements

Heartfelt thanks to my Pastor, Bishop Keith A. Butler, his lovely wife, Minister Deborah Butler, and the entire First Family, who taught me the inerrant power of the Word of God.

I want to honor and thank my family for their unending encouragement and support in everything that I do.

Special thanks to Eddie L. Robinson for writing the *Prayer of His Heart*.

Many thanks to Evangelist Marie Diggs for sharing her heart and expertise on salvation and Holy Spirit.

Thanks to Carole Stramler who was bold enough to share Jesus with me in college; my life has never been the same since.

Thank you Delmar Mays for your prayers and pronouncement of favor and success. I'll never forget it.

Treasures in Heaven

Contents

	Page
Foreword	7
Preface	9
Acknowledgements	11
Introduction	15
Why Confessions	19

Section One: Riches Revealed

Chapter 1: Proverbs Confessions	23
Chapter 2: Philippians Confessions	53
Chapter 3: Colossians Confessions	59
Chapter 4: Psalm 119 Confessions	63

Section Two: Body Benefits

Chapter 5: Healing Confessions	73

Section Three: Hidden Treasure

Chapter 6: The Names of Holy Spirit	89
Chapter 7: The Emblems of Holy Spirit	93
Chapter 8: The Power and Ability of Holy Spirit Abide in Me	97
Chapter 9: The Power and Ability of Holy Spirit Rest Upon Me	103
Chapter 10: Speaking in Tongues	105
Chapter 11: The Holy Spirit Baptism	109

Section Four: Power-Packed Prayers

Chapter 12: Model Prayers	119

Section Five: Divine Declarations

Chapter 13: There Shall Be Righteousness in the Land	133

Treasures in Heaven

Introduction

Did you know that you can turn your life around with your tongue? James 3:3-5 shows us that the tongue is to the body as a bit is to a horse, and as the rudder is to a ship. They are all very small members but they are vital keys to the direction of your entire journey!

> **James 3:3-5**
> Behold, we put bits in the horses' mouths, that they may obey us; and we turn about their whole body. Behold also the ships, which though they be so great, and are driven of fierce winds, yet are they turned about with a very small helm, whithersoever the governor listeth. Even so the tongue is a little member, and boasteth great things.

The bit in a horse's mouth causes a horse to change directions almost immediately. Some of your personal circumstances will change just as quickly. A rudder, on the other hand, cannot turn the ship immediately, because a ship is much bigger. However, the captain of the ship knows the turning process; therefore, when it doesn't yet look like the ship has changed course or even feel like it, he does not doubt that his course has indeed changed. In the same way, don't be moved by the way things in your life look right now or by the enormity of your current situation. With faith and patience, the circumstances will turn.

Treasures in Heaven

Not only do you need to know about the turning process, but also it is important to understand that what you are giving your time and attention to ends up being deposited into your heart and becomes the source of what comes out of your mouth. Out of the abundance of the heart, the mouth speaks. Keep your heart with all diligence, for out of it flows the issues of life.

> **Psalm 1:1-3**
> Blessed is the man that walketh not in the counsel of the ungodly, nor standeth in the way of sinners, nor sitteth in the seat of the scornful (ungodly or wicked). But his delight is in the law of the LORD; and in his law doth he meditate day and night. And he shall be like a tree planted by the rivers of water, that bringeth forth his fruit in his season; his leaf also shall not wither (fade); and whatsoever he doeth shall prosper.

This book makes it easy to meditate and speak the words of God day and night. You can take it with you wherever you go and use it in your time of devotion and study. It will help guide and direct you right into the perfect will of God for every area of your life. As you continue to confess the Word of God out of your mouth, you will see changes and blessings beyond measure.

> **Joshua 1:8**
> This book of the law shall not depart out of thy mouth; but thou shalt meditate therein day and night, that thou mayest observe to do according to all that is written therein: for then thou shalt make thy way prosperous, and then thou shalt have good success (or do wisely).

Introduction

May God prosper and bless you on your journey as you discover and apply all of the life-changing nuggets found in His wonderful Word.

Your friend in Christ Jesus,

Katherine E. Gardner

Treasures in Heaven

Why Confessions?

In the beginning was the Word, and the Word was with God, **and the Word was God** (John 1:1). Did you get that? The Bible doesn't just talk *about* God. The Bible *is* the Word and the Word *is* God.

> **John 1:14**
> The Word was made flesh, and dwelt among us, and we beheld his glory, the glory as of the only begotten of the Father, full of grace and truth.

Jesus is the Word. That's why it says in Hebrews 4:12 that the Word is alive and powerful. Therefore, when we confess the Word, we are confessing Jesus. When we proclaim the Word, we are proclaiming Jesus. When we believe in the Word, we are certainly believing in Jesus!

Furthermore, the Bible says in Psalm 103:20 that angels hearken to **the voice of His Word.** This literally means that the angels were created to regard, obey, and to fulfill the Word that we are giving our voices to everyday. Even more than that, words of faith will nourish you and build you up. Speaking words of faith can bring you out of despair and keep you out of oppression and depression.

> **Acts 20:32 (BBE)**
> And now, I give you into the care of God and **the word of his grace, which is able to make you strong** and to give you your heritage among all the saints.

Treasures in Heaven

1 Timothy 4:6 (RSV)
If you put these instructions before the brethren, you will be a good minister of Christ Jesus, **nourished up on the words** of faith and of the good doctrine, which you have followed.

Treasures In Heaven will make it easy for you to build yourself up by speaking words of faith concerning every area of your life. You will become stronger and stronger every single day! As you continue to confess the Word of God out of your mouth day and night, you will be changed and blessed beyond measure.

Section One
Riches Revealed

With this section, you can realize how good it is to have and to know Jesus Christ as your personal Lord and Savior. Keep in mind and recall the many benefits that are yours because of your royal relationship with the King of kings. Finally, begin to confess these benefits, privileges, and riches and then watch them manifest within your everyday life.

Treasures in Heaven

Treasures in Heaven
Chapter One

Proverbs Confessions

Day One
Proverbs Chapter One

> I know Wisdom and Instruction and I perceive the words of Understanding (1:2).
>
> I hearken unto Wisdom; therefore, I dwell securely without fear of evil (1:33).

As an introduction to the *Proverbs Confessions*, we will begin to focus on setting our hearts to know wisdom and to perceive the words of understanding. The word "know" in Proverbs 1:2 means to be acquainted with; to observe, discern, discover, regard or have respect unto. The word "perceive" in that same verse means to separate mentally or to distinguish. In verse 33, the word "hearken" means to hear intelligently with implication of attention and obedience. When you say that you know wisdom and instruction, this is the confession that you are really making:

I am acquainted with wisdom and instruction; I observe and discern it. I can distinguish words of understanding from words of foolishness. I not only have respect unto wisdom, but also I apply wisdom principles to my everyday life.

Day Two
Proverbs Chapter Two

I bow down my ear unto wisdom and I apply my heart to understanding (2:2).

I cry after knowledge and lift up my voice for understanding (2:3).

I search for wisdom as for hidden treasures (2:4).

I understand the fear of the Lord and find the knowledge of God (2:5).

The Lord gives me wisdom and from his mouth I get knowledge and understanding (2:6).

God lays up sound wisdom for me and the Lord is a shield unto me (2:7).

He guards the paths of justice and preserves my way (2:8).

I understand righteousness and justice, equity; yes every good path (2:9).

Discretion will watch over me; understanding will guard me (2:11).

I walk in the way of good men and keep the
paths of righteousness (2:20).

Today the focus is on stretching out and actively and diligently seeking out knowledge and understanding from the Lord. The word used for "search" in Proverbs 2:4 means to search out by any method, specifically in worship or prayer; by implication, to strive after; ask, beg, beseech, desire, enquire, get, make inquisition, procure, (make) request, require, seek (for). In other words, you are making your heartfelt request for wisdom and knowledge known unto God. Through your diligent search of the Word of God and the ways of God, you are acknowledging that you can't afford to go about your daily functions in life without His mind on the matter.

Day Three
Proverbs Chapter Three

Length of days, long life, and abundant welfare
are continually added unto me (3:2).

I bind Loyalty and Faithfulness around my neck
and write them on the table of my heart (3:3).

I have favor and good understanding in the sight
of God and man (3:4).

I trust in the Lord with all my heart and I lean not
to my own understanding (3:5).

I do not rely on my own insight (3:5).

In all my ways I acknowledge the Lord, and he
directs my paths (3:6).

I keep sound wisdom and discretion and I will not let them escape from before my eyes (3:21).

I walk on my way securely and my foot does not stumble (3:23).

The Lord is my confidence and He keeps my foot from being caught (3:26).

I am wise and I inherit glory and honor (3:35).

Today you are celebrating some of the benefits of acknowledging the Lord in all of your ways!

Day Four
Proverbs Chapter Four

I prize wisdom highly, and she exalts me; Wisdom honors me because I embrace her (4:8).

Wisdom gives to me a crown of glory, and an ornament of grace to my head (4:9).

As I walk, my steps shall not be hampered; As I run, I will not stumble (4:12).

I keep hold of instruction and will not let go, because she is my life (4:13).

I avoid, turn away from, and pass on from the path of the wicked (4:14).

Chapter 1 ~ Proverbs Confessions

My path is like the light of dawn, which shines brighter and brighter unto the perfect day (4:18).

I keep my heart with all diligence because out of it flow the issues of my life (4:23).

My eyes look directly forward, and my gaze is straight before me looking unto Jesus, the Author and the Finisher of my faith (4:25; Hebrews 12:2).

I take heed to the path of my feet, so that all my ways are sure (4:26).

I swerve not to the right nor to the left; I turn my foot away from evil (4:27).

Focus on guarding your heart and taking heed to protect the wisdom that has been deposited there by God.

Day Five
Proverbs Chapter Five

I am as a loving hind and a graceful doe unto my husband (5:19).

My affection satisfies him at all times (5:19).

My husband is infatuated with my love at all times (5:19).

If you are married or preparing to be married, focus on the fact that God has anointed you and empowered you to satisfy your spouse (or future spouse) like no other. He is the God who is more than enough and He will help you to be more than enough for your mate. You are an abundant overflow for your mate!

Day Six

Continue to seek out and meditate on how you can be a blessing to your loved ones.

Day Seven
Proverbs Chapter Seven

> Wisdom is my sister and Insight is my intimate friend (7:4).

Focus on the fact that the wisdom of God will be with you for life. It's in you.

Day Eight
Proverbs Chapter Eight

> My mouth speaks the truth because wickedness is an abomination to my lips (8:7).
>
> All the words of my mouth are righteous; there is nothing twisted or crooked in them (8:8).
>
> I have counsel and I have sound wisdom (8:14).
>
> I have insight and I have strength (8:14).
>
> Riches and honor are with me, yes, enduring wealth and prosperity (8:18).

I walk in the way of righteousness and in the paths of justice (8:20).

I am endowed with wealth, and my treasuries are continually being filled (8:21).

A wise man or woman is known by what he or she says or does not say; and by what he or she does or does not do. Also, others can see the results of wisdom because it causes you to obtain riches and honor.

Day Nine

Focus on speaking and acting with wisdom in every situation and circumstance that you face today.

Day Ten
Proverbs Chapter Ten

I have a diligent hand and it makes me rich (10:4).

I walk in integrity; therefore, I walk in security (10:9).

My mouth is a fountain of life (10:11).

My love covers all offenses (10:12).

Wisdom is found on my lips because I have understanding (10:13).

I continually lay up knowledge (10:14).

I heed Instruction; therefore, I stay on the path of life (10:17).

Treasures in Heaven

I restrain my lips because when my words are many: sin is not lacking (10:19).

My tongue **is** choice silver (10:20).

My lips feed many souls (10:21).

The Blessing of the Lord makes me rich, and he adds no sorrow with it (10:22).

Wise conduct is pleasure to me because I am a woman of understanding, but it is like a game to a fool to do wrong (10:23).

I am a righteous woman and my desire shall be granted (10:24).

I am established forever (10:25).

My hope and expectation ends in gladness and will not perish (10:28).

I am upright and the Way of the Lord is strength to me (10:29).

I am the just and my mouth brings forth wisdom (10:31).

I am the righteous and my lips know what is acceptable (10:32).

Many people are starving to hear a kind and encouraging word from someone. Let your words feed others today.

Chapter 1 ~ Proverbs Confessions

Day Eleven
Proverbs Chapter Eleven

I am upright and integrity shall continually guide me (11:3).

Righteousness directs my way and keeps it straight (11:5).

I am upright and righteousness shall deliver me (11:6).

I am a gracious woman and I retain honor (11:16).

My husband is a strong man and he retains riches (11:16).

I sow righteousness and my reward is sure (11:18).

I am upright in my ways; therefore, I am the Lord's delight (11:20).

I am a beautiful woman with much discretion (11:22).

I am kind, benefiting myself, but a cruel man hurts himself (11:17).

Our righteousness comes from God when we acknowledge Jesus Christ as our Lord and Savior. However, here the focus is on our living a moral and upright life. We don't live this lifestyle because we are trying to earn salvation, but in gratitude because we have already been saved by grace (see section on salvation).

Day Twelve
Proverbs Chapter Twelve

I love discipline because he who hates correction is stupid (12:1).

I am righteous and my roots will never be moved (12:3).

I am a virtuous woman; I am a good wife (12:4).

I am a crown of glory to my husband (12:4).

My thoughts are pure and just (12:5).

The house of the righteous shall stand; therefore, my house shall stand (12:7).

I am satisfied with good from the fruit of my words and the work of my hands (12:14).

I ignore an insult, but a fool's wrath is quickly known (12:16).

My tongue brings healing because rash words are like the piercing of a sword (12:18).

I plan good and I have joy (12:20).

No evil shall befall me, but the wicked are filled with trouble (12:21).

I deal truthfully and faithfully; therefore, I am the Lord's delight (12:22).

My diligent hand will rule (12:24).

I am a diligent woman; therefore, I shall get precious wealth (12:27).

In my path is only life (12:28).

Focus on remaining teachable and pliable in the hands of God.

Day Thirteen
Proverbs Chapter Thirteen

I eat good from the fruit of my mouth (13:2).

I guard my mouth; therefore, I preserve my life, because he who opens wide his lips shall come to ruin (13:3).

I take advice, because strife and contention comes by pride (13:10).

Wisdom wins favor on my behalf (13:15).

I am a reserved woman and I act with knowledge (13:16).

I heed correction; therefore, I am honored (13:18).

I walk with wise men, because a companion of fools will be destroyed (13:20).

I am righteous and prosperity is my reward (13:21).

I have a good husband who lays up an inheritance to his children's children (13:22).

The Lord corrects those whom He loves. A part of wisdom is being able to keep a good attitude when being corrected and learning from your mistakes.

Day Fourteen
Proverbs Chapter Fourteen

I build my house, but the foolish woman tears it down with her own hands (14:1).

I walk in uprightness because I fear the Lord, but he who is devious in his ways despises the Lord (14:2).

I am wise and cautious, turning away from evil, because only a fool throws off restraint and is careless (14:16).

I am patient and a woman of discretion, because he that is quick to get angry acts foolishly (14:17).

I am crowned with knowledge (14:18).

I devise good and I am rewarded with loyalty and faithfulness (14:22).

Wisdom is a crown unto me (14:24).

I have strong confidence in the fear of the Lord; therefore, my children will have a refuge (14:26).

I am slow to anger, because I have great understanding (14:29).

My mind is sound and tranquil, which gives life to my flesh (14:30).

Wisdom abides in my mind (14:33).

Focus on peace today—peace of mind and heart as well as peace with God and others. It is wise to let the peace of God rule and reign in your heart. It is also wise to seek peace in your dealings with others.

Day Fifteen
Proverbs Chapter Fifteen

I turn away wrath by giving soft answers, because harsh words only stir up anger (15:1).

My tongue is wise and dispenses knowledge (15:2).

My tongue is gentle as a wholesome tree of life (15:4).

Much treasure abides in my house (15:6).

My lips spread knowledge (15:7).

My prayer is the Lord's delight (15:8).

I pursue righteousness; therefore, the Lord loves me (15:9).

My heart is glad therefore my countenance is cheerful (15:13).

I am slow to anger, which quiets contention, but a hot-temper only stirs up strife (15:18).

My way is made plain before me (15:19).

I speak words in due season, and how good it is! (15:23)

Treasures in Heaven

My path only leads upward to life (15:24).

My words are pure and pleasing to the Lord (15:26).

My heart and mind studies and ponders how I should answer (15:28).

Focus on being slow to speak, quick to listen, and slow to get angry. When you do speak or give an answer, be aware of the effect it may have upon the hearers.

Day Sixteen
Proverbs Chapter Sixteen

I commit my works unto the Lord and my thoughts and plans shall be established (16:3).

My ways please the Lord and he makes even my enemies to be at peace with me (16:7).

My mind plans my way, but the Lord directs my steps (16:9).

I am wise and can appease the wrath of a king (16:14).

I handle and understand matters wisely; therefore, I prosper and find good (16:20).

I am wise in heart and I shall be called a woman of discernment (16:21).

My pleasant speech increases persuasiveness (16:21).

Chapter 1 ~ Proverbs Confessions

My heart is wise and it teaches my mouth what to speak, when to speak, and how to speak, so that what I say is proper, pertinent, and seasonable; adding to it the strength of reason (16:23).

My words are pleasant like a honeycomb, sweet to the soul and health to the body (16:24).

I am slow to anger; therefore, I am better than the mighty (16:32).

I keep rule over my spirit; therefore, I am better than one who takes a city (16:32).

Continue to focus on your responses and reactions in different situations and circumstances. No one benefits from intense arguments and debates. Applied wisdom in this area can persuade kings to see things differently.

Day Seventeen
Proverbs Chapter Seventeen

I forgive offenses because I seek love (17:9).

I shut my mouth before a quarrel breaks out because the beginning of strife is like letting out water (17:14).

I am a good friend who loves at all times (17:17).

My heart is merry and cheerful, which is a good medicine unto my body (17:22).

I am a woman of understanding and I set my face toward wisdom (17:24).

> I have knowledge and an excellent and cool spirit; therefore, I spare my words (17:27).

Jesus said that the peacemakers are blessed. Strive to live at peace with all men and to be the peacemaker in your workplace.

Day Eighteen
Proverbs Chapter Eighteen

> My gift makes room for me and brings me before great men (18:16).
>
> Death and life are in the power of my tongue (18:21).
>
> I love to speak life so I will eat of its fruits (18:21).
>
> I always show myself friendly (18:24).

Know that you are unique and special. Give of something that you have today that will be a blessing unto others. When you are a giver and you give out of who you are, you will be bought before great men, including your husband!

Day Nineteen
Proverbs Chapter Nineteen

> I get wisdom and keep understanding; therefore, I shall prosper and find good (19:8).
>
> I am slow to anger, because I have good sense (19:11).

I overlook an offense, and it is to my glory to do so (19:11).

I do not quarrel, because a quarreling wife is as a continual dripping (19:13).

I am meek and quiet; A Virtuous Wife (19:14).

I am a choice gift of God to my husband (19:14).

I listen to advise and accept instruction (19:20).

I gain Wisdom for the future (19:20).

Only the purpose of the Lord for my life shall stand and be established (19:21).

Know that God's purpose for your life will be accomplished as you continue to seek his face and acknowledge Him in all that you do.

Day Twenty
Proverbs Chapter Twenty

I cease from strife because it is an honor for me to do so (20:3).

My husband and I walk in integrity; therefore, our children are blessed after us (20:7).

My lips of knowledge are a precious jewel (20:15).

I do not avenge myself (20:22).

> I wait on the Lord and He saves me, protects me, and pleads my cause (20:22).
>
> My steps are ordered of the Lord (20:24).
>
> The glory of my man (young men) is his strength (20:29).

Know that your steps are ordered of the Lord. The word "steps" means companions. Did you know that God wants to lead you into right companionships? God is concerned about the people in your life. He wants you to have wise and godly companions.

Day Twenty-One
Proverbs Chapter Twenty-One

> I am diligent and my plans surely lead to abundance (21:5).
>
> My conduct is pure and right (21:8).
>
> I pursue righteousness and kindness; therefore, I find life and honor (21:21).
>
> I guard my mouth and keep my tongue; therefore, I stay out of trouble (21:23).
>
> I am a giver and I don't hold back, because I am the righteous (21:26).

Jesus said, "When you've seen Me, you've seen My Father." When others see you, can they see the resemblance of God, your Father?

Day Twenty-Two
Proverbs Chapter Twenty-Two

I choose a good name and favor rather than great riches (22:1).

I am humble and I fear the Lord; therefore, my reward is riches, honor, and life (22:4).

I love and esteem purity of heart and my speech is full of grace (22:11).

I bow down my ear and hear the words of the wise and keep them ready on my lips (22:17,18).

I am diligent in business; therefore, I will stand before kings (22:29).

Being upright before God and man has its rewards. Choose a good name and reputation as being better than riches, and then riches will come.

Day Twenty-Three
Proverbs Chapter Twenty-Three

As I think in my heart so am I (23:7).

My Redeemer lives and He is strong, and He is the One who pleads my cause (23:11).

My lips speak right things (23:16).

Surely I have a future, and my hope will **not** be cut off (23:18).

God sees you as precious and valuable. We like to sing songs to God that declares there is none like Him. However, God declares that there is none like you! Agree with God today.

Day Twenty-Four
Proverbs Chapter Twenty-Four

> By Wisdom my house is built, and by Understanding it is established (24:3)
>
> By Knowledge my rooms are filled with all precious and pleasant riches (24:4).
>
> My husband is wise; therefore, he is mightier than a strong man (24:5).
>
> I have a man of knowledge; who is greater than he who has strength (24:5).
>
> My strength is **big**; therefore, I will not faint in the day of adversity (24:10).
>
> Wisdom is like honey to my soul; It is good and sweet to my taste (24:13-14).
>
> Even when I fall seven times, I always rise again because I am the righteous (24:16).

Marriage and family were God's ideas. Through Him, two imperfect individuals can come together as one and still have a very successful and satisfying home life.

Day Twenty-Five
Proverbs Chapter Twenty-Five

My words are fitly spoken like apples of gold in settings of silver (25:11).

I am a faithful messenger and I refresh the spirit of my master (25:13).

I have great patience to bear the present heat without being taken in by it; I wait for a fit opportunity to offer my reasons and give others time to consider them. By this, even a prince may be persuaded; how much more a common man (25:15).

My tongue is soft and it soothes the roughest of spirits and overcomes even those that are most severe and ill tempered (25:15).

I do not overeat, but I eat only what is sufficient for me (25:16).

I am a woman of self-control (25:28).

Focus on moderation and self-control today. As you grow in these areas, the quality of your life will greatly increase.

Day Twenty-Six
Proverbs Chapter Twenty-Six

I will not answer a fool according to his folly, lest I become like him and he becomes wise in his own eyes (26:4,5).

A contentious woman is as a continual dripping; therefore, I am not contentious (27:15).

Determine not to be pulled into arguments today. In other words, "Don't even go there!"

Day Twenty-Seven

Learn to identify the "buttons" within yourself that others like to push to get your feathers ruffled. Start desensitizing those areas with the Word of God.

Day Twenty-Eight
Proverbs Chapter Twenty-Eight

I seek the Lord; therefore, I understand all things (28:5).

I am upright; therefore, I shall have good things in my possession (28:10).

I confess and forsake my sins; therefore, I obtain mercy, but he who hardens his heart will fall into calamity (28:14).

I am a faithful woman; therefore, I abound in blessings (28:20).

I trust in the Lord, therefore I shall be enriched (28:25).

I trust not in my own heart or mind, but I walk in the Wisdom of God, and I am always delivered (28:26).

It's so sweet to trust in Jesus! Focus on God's ability and not your own. Then cast all your cares on Him.

Day Twenty-Nine
Proverbs Chapter Twenty-Nine

I am a righteous woman; therefore, I sing and rejoice in the Lord (29:6).

I am wise, because I turn away from wrath and arguments (29:8).

I run with the vision; therefore, I will not perish (29:18).

I am blessed, because I obey the Word of God (29:18).

I am humble in spirit; therefore, I obtain honor, but pride will bring a man low (29:23).

I trust in the Lord and I am safe (29:25).

Bless the Lord today and remember all of His benefits.

Day Thirty
Proverbs Chapter Thirty

I put my trust in the Lord and He is a shield unto me (30:5).

If others could physically see God walking along side you today, how would the atmosphere change when you come around? Always remember God is on your side, and He is your shield.

Day Thirty-One
Chapter Thirty-One

I am a Virtuous Woman and a Good Wife (31:10).

My price is far above rubies (31:10).

The heart of my husband safely trusts in me (31:11).

My husband has no lack of gain (31:11).

I do my husband good, and not harm, all the days of my life (31:12).

I work willingly with my hands, serving my family with gladness of heart (31:13-16).

I keep my body strong and fit (31:17).

My husband is known in the gates when he sits among the elders of the land (31:23).

Strength and Honor are my clothing (31:25).

I keep watch over my household, and I do not eat the bread of idleness (31:27).

My children rise up and call me blessed (31:28).

My husband praises me because a woman who fears the Lord is to be praised (31:28,30).

Chapter 1 ~ Proverbs Confessions

God's "super" on your "natural" makes you a beautiful, powerful, supernatural woman of God!

Treasures of a Man From Proverbs

There is no man like a man of God. He stands tall in the land. He is a man of honor. He is a man of passion, purpose, and power. His heart is open and yielded to God Almighty.

> I keep my way far from a loose woman, and do not go near the door of her house, lest I be full of grief at the end of my life when my flesh and my body are wasted (5:8,11).
>
> I drink waters out of my own cistern, and running waters out of my own well (5:15).
>
> I let my fountain be blessed, and rejoice in the wife of my youth (5:18).
>
> My wife is as a loving hind and a graceful doe unto me (5:19).
>
> Her breasts satisfy me at all times (5:19).
>
> My passion is moved by her love at all times (5:19).
>
> Wisdom is my sister and Insight is my intimate friend; they keep me from the loose woman, even from her whose words are smooth – for many strong men have been slain by her (7:4,5,26).
>
> I am a righteous man and my desire shall be granted (10:24).
>
> I am established forever (10:25).

Chapter 1 ~ Proverbs Confessions

My wife is a gracious woman and she retains honor (11:16).

I am a strong man and I retains riches (11:16).

I am a merciful man, because a cruel man only hurts himself (11:17).

I am a lover of training and knowledge (12:1).

I am a good man who obtains favor from the Lord (12:2).

I am a righteous man and my roots will never be moved (12:3).

My virtuous woman is a crown unto me (12:4).

I am a diligent man; therefore, I shall get much wealth (12:27).

I am sharp and I do everything with knowledge, but a fool makes known his folly (13:16).

I heed correction; therefore, I am honored (13:18).

I walk with wise men, because a companion of fools will be destroyed (13:20).

I am a good husband who lays up an inheritance to my children's children (13:22).

I am a man of good sense; I am crowned with knowledge (14:18).

Treasures in Heaven

My mind plans my way, but the Lord directs my steps (16:9).

I am a wise man and can pacify the wrath of a king (16:14).

I am a man of understanding and I set my face toward wisdom (17:24).

My wife is a choice gift of God (19:14).

Only the purpose of the Lord for my life shall stand and be established (19:21).

My wife and I walk in integrity, therefore our children are blessed after us (20:7).

I am diligent and my plans surely lead to abundance (21:5).

I choose a good name and favor rather than great riches (22:1).

Even when I fall seven times, I always rise again because I am a righteous man (24:16).

I have great patience (25:15).

I speak with wisdom (25:15).

I am a man of self-control (25:28).

I am a faithful man; therefore, I abound in blessings (28:20).

Chapter 1 ~ Proverbs Confessions

I trust in the Lord; therefore, I shall be enriched in all things (28:25).

My wife is a virtuous woman (31:10).

Her price is far above rubies (31:10).

My heart safely trusts in her (31:11).

I have no lack of gain (31:11).

My wife does me good, and not harm, all the days of her life (31:12).

Strength and Honor are her clothing (31:25).

My children rise up and call her blessed (31:28).

I praise my wife, because a woman who fears the Lord is to be praised (31:28,30).

Treasures in Heaven

Treasures in Heaven
Chapter Two

Philippians Confessions

As you study the books of Philippians and Colossians, these Scriptures will become a part of you, and your desires will begin to change. As a mature believer, you will have a strong desire to make sure that your gentleness is known to all men. In other words, you will strive to let the life and character of Jesus Christ shine brightly so that others will come to the glorious light of the gospel.

Philippians Chapter One

I have grace and peace unto me from God my Father, and from my Lord Jesus Christ (1:2).

I am confident that he which hath begun a good work in me will perform it until the day of Jesus Christ (1:6).

Today my love abounds yet more and even more in knowledge and all judgment (1:9).

Today I approve things that are excellent (1:10).

I am sincere and without offense till the day of Christ (1:10).

I am being filled with the fruits of righteousness by Jesus Christ, unto the glory and praise of God (1:11).

I am bold to speak the Word of God without fear today (1:14).

I will in no way be put to shame (1:20).

With all boldness Christ will be magnified in my body (1:20).

I will only let my conversation be worthy of the gospel (1:27).

Philippians Chapter Two

I let nothing be done through strife (rivalry) or vainglory (conceit) (2:3).

In all humility, I esteem others as better than myself (2:3).

I not only look on my own things, but I look on the things of others (2:4).

I let the same mind be in me which was also in Christ Jesus (2:5).

Chapter 2 ~ Philippians Confessions

I make myself of no reputation, taking on the form of a servant (2:7).

I humble myself and become obedient even unto death (2:8).

It is God working in me both to will and to do of his good pleasure (2:13).

I will do all things without complaining and arguing (2:14).

I'm blameless and sincere, without blemish (2:15).

I shine as a light in the midst of a crooked and perverse nation (2:15).

I hold forth the Word of Life, that I may rejoice in the day of Christ (2:16).

I do not run or labor in vain (2:16).

Philippians Chapter Three

I worship God in the spirit and rejoice in Christ Jesus (3:3).

I have no confidence in the flesh (3:3).

I am found in Him, not having my own righteousness (3:9).

My righteousness is from God by faith (3:9).

I know Him, and the power of His resurrection, and the fellowship of His sufferings (3:10).

I press on to take hold of that which I was taken hold of by Jesus (3:12).

I purposely forget those things which are behind (3:13).

I stretch forward to the things which are before me (3:13).

I press toward the mark for the prize of the high calling of God in Christ Jesus (3:14).

Philippians Chapter Four

I stand fast in the Lord (4:1).

I rejoice in the Lord always (4:4).

I let my gentleness be known unto all men for the Lord is at hand (4:5).

I am not careful or anxious for anything (4:6).

In every thing, by prayer and supplication with thanksgiving, I make my requests known unto God (4:6).

I let the peace of God keep my heart and mind through Christ Jesus (4:7).

I focus on and think only about things that are true, honest, just, pure, lovely, and of good report; if there is any virtue, and if there be any praise, I think on these things (4:8).

Chapter 2 ~ Philippians Confessions

I do only those things which I have learned, received, and heard from the Lord: (4:9).

The God of peace shall be with me (4:9).

I have learned, in whatever state I am, therewith to be content (4:11).

I can do all things through Christ which strengthens me (4:13).

I am a giver and I have fruit that abounds to my account (4:17).

I have all, and abound; I am full (4:18).

My God supplies all my need according to His riches in glory by Christ Jesus (4:19).

The grace of my Lord Jesus Christ is with me always (4:23).

Treasures in Heaven

Treasures in Heaven
Chapter Three

Colossians Confessions

Colossians Chapter One

I am filled with the knowledge of God's will in all wisdom and spiritual understanding (1:9).

I walk worthy of the Lord unto all pleasing (1:10).

I am fruitful in every good work (1:10).

I am increasing in the knowledge of God (1:10).

I am strengthened with all might, according to God's glorious power, unto all patience and longsuffering with joy (1:11).

I am delivered from the power of darkness (1:13).

I have redemption through the blood (1:14).

I have forgiveness of sins through the blood (1:14).

I have peace through the blood (1:20).

I continue grounded and steadfast in the faith (1:23).

I am not moved away from the hope of the gospel (1:23).

I am made a minister, which is given to me for others, to fulfill the Word of God (1:25).

I have Christ in me, the hope of glory (1:27).

I strive according to His working, which works in me mightily (1:29).

Colossians Chapter Two

I have received Christ Jesus as Lord, so I walk in him (2:6).

I am rooted and built up in Christ (2:7).

I am established in the faith, abounding therein with thanksgiving (2:7).

I am complete and made whole in Christ, which is the head of all principality and power (2:10).

I am holding firmly by joints and bands to Christ, the Head, having all my nourishment supplied (2:19a).

I increase with the increase of God (2:19b).

Chapter 3 ~ Colossians Confessions

Colossians Chapter Three

I have been raised together with Christ; therefore, I seek those things which are above (3:1).

I set my affection (mind) on things above, not on things on the earth (3:2).

My life is hid with Christ in God (3:3).

I deny fornication, uncleanness, lustful passion, evil desire, and the love of the world, which is spiritual idolatry (3:5).

I also put off anger, wrath, malice, slander, and filthy communication out of my mouth (3:8).

I lie not to others (3:9).

I have put off the old man with his deeds (3:9).

I put on the new man, which is renewed in knowledge after the image of my Creator (3:10).

I put on therefore, as the elect of God, holy and beloved, bowels of mercies, kindness, humbleness of mind, meekness, longsuffering (3:12).

I am forbearing others, and forgiving others even as Christ has forgiven me (3:13).

Above all these things, I put on love, which is the bond of perfection (3:14).

I let the peace of God rule in my heart (3:15).

I let the word of Christ dwell in me richly in all wisdom (3:16).

Whatever I do in word or deed, I do all in the name of Jesus (3:17).

Whatsoever I do, I do it heartily, as unto the Lord, and not unto men (3:23).

I receive the reward of the inheritance of the Lord (3:24).

Colossians Chapter Four

I continue in prayer, and watch in the same with thanksgiving (4:2).

God opens up unto me a door of utterance to speak the Word of God (4:3).

I walk in wisdom toward them that are without (4:5).

I am redeeming the time (4:5).

My speech is always with grace, seasoned with salt (4:6a).

I know how I ought to answer every man (4:6b).

I labor fervently for myself and others in prayer (4:12).

I stand perfect and complete in all the will of God (4:12).

I also take heed to my ministry which I have received in the Lord, that I fulfill it (4:17).

Treasures in Heaven
Chapter Four

Psalm 119 Nuggets

God the Father called David a man after His own heart. David had a heart that longed for the things of God. Throughout the book of Psalms, David placed his highest priority on prayer and communion with God. He greatly esteemed the Word of God and cried out for knowledge and understanding of Godly principles.

Continue to make known your hunger and thirst for the presence of God and for understanding of His Word. He is pleased to give you the desires of your heart and to satisfy you with all good things. You are a man or woman after God's own heart!

> With my whole heart have I sought thee: O let me not wander from thy commandments (119:10).

> Thy word have I hid in mine heart, that I might not sin against thee (Psalm 119:11).

Treasures in Heaven

With my lips have I declared all the laws of thy mouth (Psalm 119:13).

I have rejoiced in the way of thy decrees, as much as in all riches (Psalm 119:14).

I will meditate in thy precepts, and have respect unto thy ways (Psalm 119:15).

I will delight myself in thy statutes: I will not forget thy word (Psalm 119:16).

Open thou mine eyes, that I may behold wondrous things out of thy law (Psalm 119:18).

My soul breaketh for the longing that it hath unto thy judgments at all times (Psalm 119:20).

Your unchanging Word is my delight and the guide of my footsteps (Psalm 119:24).

Teach me, O Lord, the way of thy principles; and I shall keep it unto the end (Psalm 119:33).

Give me understanding, and I shall obey thy law; yea, I shall observe it with my whole heart (Psalm 119:34).

Make me to go in the path of thy commandments; for therein do I delight (Psalm 119:35).

Incline my heart unto thy Word, and not to selfish desires (Psalm 119:36).

Turn away mine eyes from beholding vanity; and quicken thou me in thy way (Psalm 119:37).

Chapter 4 ~ Psalm 119 Confessions

Stablish thy word unto thy servant, who is devoted to thy honor (Psalm 119:38).

Behold, I have longed after thy precepts: quicken me in thy righteousness (Psalm 119:40).

And I will delight myself in thy commandments, which I have loved (Psalm 119:47).

My hands also will I lift up unto thy commandments, which I have loved; and I will meditate in thy statutes (Psalms 119:48).

Thou art my portion, O Lord: I have said that I would keep thy words (Psalm 119:57).

I have given my mind to do thy pleasure with my whole heart: be merciful unto me according to thy word (Psalm 119:58).

At midnight I will rise to give thanks unto thee because of thy righteous judgments (Psalm 119:62).

Teach me good judgment and knowledge: For I have believed thy commandments (Psalm 119:66).

The law of thy mouth is better unto me than thousands of gold and silver (Psalm 119:72).

Thy hands have made me and fashioned me: give me understanding, that I may learn thy commandments (Psalm 119:73).

Let those that fear thee turn unto me, and those that have known thy decrees (Psalm 119:79).

Treasures in Heaven

Let my heart be sound in thy principles; that I be not ashamed (Psalm 119:80).

O how I love thy law! It is my meditation all the day (Psalm 119:97).

How sweet are thy words unto my taste! Yea, sweeter than honey to my mouth (Psalm 119:103)!

Thy word is a lamp unto my feet, and a light unto my path (Psalm 119:105).

I am thy servant; give me understanding that I may know thy testimonies (Psalm 119:125).

Therefore I love thy commandments above gold; yea, above fine gold (Psalm 119:127).

Therefore I esteem all thy precepts concerning all things to be right; and I hate every false way (Psalm 119:128).

The entrance of thy words giveth light; it giveth understanding unto the simple (Psalm 119:130).

I opened my mouth, and panted: for I longed for thy commandments (Psalm 119:131).

Order my steps in thy word: and let not any iniquity have dominion over me (Psalm119:133).

Make thy face to shine upon thy servant; and teach me thy principles (Psalm 119:135).

Thy word is very pure: therefore thy servant loveth it (Psalm 119:140).

Chapter 4 ~ Psalm 119 Confessions

I rejoice at thy word, as one that findeth great wealth (Psalm 119:162).

I hate and abhor lying: but thy law do I love (Psalm 119:163).

Seven times a day do I praise thee because of thy righteous judgments (Psalm 119:164).

Great peace have they which love thy law: and nothing shall offend them (Psalm 119:165).

My lips shall utter praise, when thou hast taught me thy statutes (Psalm 119:171).

My tongue shall speak of thy word: for all thy commandments are righteous (Psalm 119:172).

Let thine hand help me; for I have chosen thy ways (Psalm 119:173).

I have longed for thy salvation, O Lord; and thy law is my delight (Psalm 119:174).

Treasure Chest

Did you know that the angels are listening for words of God spoken from your mouth, so that they can hasten to perform it? Think of current situations in your life right now that you want to see changed. What does God's Word say about your current situation? He wants the very best for you just as a natural parent wants for their children. Now create your own personal confessions that declare the final outcome you desire.

Situation:

Scripture References:

Personal Confession:

Situation:

Scripture References:

Treasures in Heaven

Personal Confession:

Situation:

Scripture References:

Personal Confession:

Treasures in Heaven

Section Two
Body Benefits

If you were to go on a paid shopping spree at your favorite store, would you pick out what you wanted and then leave the store without your bags? Of course you wouldn't!

Jesus paid an expensive price for your healing. Divine health and healing now belong to you. Don't leave this earth without taking what is yours. Dare to believe it. Say what you believe, and then thank God Almighty for paying the price for you to receive it.

Treasures in Heaven

Treasures in Heaven
Chapter Five

Healing Confessions

Jesus paid the price for my healing; By His stripes I am healed.

> **1 Peter 2:24**
> Who his own self bare our sins in his own body on (to) the tree, that we, being dead to sins, should live unto righteousness: by whose stripes ye were healed.

I am healthy, wealthy, and whole, in Jesus name.

> **3 John 2**
> Beloved, I wish (pray) above all things that thou mayest prosper and be in health, even as thy soul prospereth.

Jesus is the Lord of my life, and the Healer of my body.

> **Exodus 15:26**
> If thou wilt diligently hearken to the voice of the LORD thy God, and wilt do that which is right in

Treasures in Heaven

his sight, and wilt give ear to his commandments, and keep all his statutes, I will put none of these diseases upon thee, which I have brought upon the Egyptians: for I am the LORD that healeth thee.

I am a servant of the Most High God, and He takes sickness away from me and my family.

Exodus 23:25
And ye shall serve the LORD your God, and he shall bless thy bread, and thy water; and I will take sickness away from the midst of thee.

I bless the Lord at all times. He heals every one of my diseases.

Psalm 103:2-3
Bless the LORD, O my soul, and forget not all his benefits: Who forgiveth all thine iniquities; who healeth all thy diseases.

I am delivered, set free, and healed by the Word of God.

Psalm 107:20
He sent his word, and healed them, and delivered them from their destructions.

The Word is working a healing and a cure in my body right now, even as I speak the Word of God out of my mouth.

Proverbs 4:20-22
My son, attend to my words; incline thine ear unto my sayings. Let them not depart from thine eyes; keep them in the midst of thine

Chapter 5 ~ Healing Confessions

heart. For they are life unto those that find them, and health (medicine) to all their flesh.

God has given me the good and perfect gift of divine health and healing.

James 1:17
Every good gift and every perfect gift is from above, and cometh down from the Father of lights, with whom is no variableness, neither shadow of turning.

I belong to God Almighty and I resist sin, sickness, and disease.

James 4:7
Submit yourselves therefore to God. Resist the devil, and he will flee from you.

I minister healing to the sick and they do recover according to the Word of God.

Mark 16:18
They shall take up serpents; and if they drink any deadly thing, it shall not hurt them; they shall lay hands on the sick, and they shall recover.

Jesus took my sickness and bore my pain on the cross, so that I don't have to live with it.

Matthew 8:17
That it might be fulfilled which was spoken by Esaias the prophet, saying, Himself took our infirmities, and bare our sicknesses.

Jesus is the same Healer today as He was yesterday when He healed the multitudes.

> **Hebrews 13:8**
> Jesus Christ the same yesterday, and to day, and for ever.

> **Matthew 4:23**
> And Jesus went about all Galilee, teaching in their synagogues, and preaching the gospel of the kingdom, and healing all manner of sickness and all manner of disease among the people.

I am redeemed from sickness by the blood of the Lamb.

> **1 Peter 1:18-19**
> Forasmuch as ye know that ye were not redeemed with corruptible things, as silver and gold, from your vain conversation received by tradition from your fathers; But with the precious blood of Christ, as of a lamb without blemish and without spot.

Jesus redeemed me from the curse of sickness and disease.

> **Galatians 3:13**
> Christ hath redeemed us from the curse of the law, being made a curse for us: for it is written, Cursed is every one that hangeth on a tree.

Abraham's blessing is mine.

> **Deuteronomy 28:1-14**
> And it shall come to pass, if thou shalt hearken

Chapter 5 ~ Healing Confessions

diligently unto the voice of the LORD thy God, to observe and to do all his commandments which I command thee this day, that the LORD thy God will set thee on high above all nations of the earth:

And all these blessings shall come on thee, and overtake thee, if thou shalt hearken unto the voice of the LORD thy God (2).

Blessed shalt thou be in the city, and blessed shalt thou be in the field (3).

Blessed shall be the fruit of thy body, and the fruit of thy ground, and the fruit of thy cattle, the increase of thy kine, and the flocks of thy sheep (4).

Blessed shall be thy basket and thy store [dough or kneading troughs] {5}

Blessed shalt thou be when thou comest in, and blessed shalt thou be when thou goest out (6).

The LORD shall cause thine enemies that rise up against thee to be smitten before thy face: they shall come out against thee one way, and flee before thee seven ways (7).

The LORD shall command the blessing upon thee in thy storehouses (barns), and in all that thou settest thine hand unto; and he shall bless thee in the land which the LORD thy God giveth thee (8).

The LORD shall establish thee an holy people

Treasures in Heaven

unto himself, as he hath sworn unto thee, if thou shalt keep the commandments of the LORD thy God, and walk in his ways (9).

And all people of the earth shall see that thou art called by the name of the LORD; and they shall be afraid of thee (10).

And the LORD shall make thee plenteous in goods (for good), in the fruit of thy body (belly), and in the fruit of thy cattle, and in the fruit of thy ground, in the land which the LORD sware unto thy fathers to give thee (11).

The LORD shall open unto thee his good treasure, the heaven to give the rain unto thy land in his season, and to bless all the work of thine hand: and thou shalt lend unto many nations, and thou shalt not borrow (12).

And the LORD shall make thee the head, and not the tail; and thou shalt be above only, and thou shalt not be beneath; if that thou hearken unto the commandments of the LORD thy God, which I command thee this day, to observe and to do them (13):

And thou shalt not go aside from any of the words which I command thee this day, to the right hand, or to the left, to go after other gods to serve them (14).

I am the seed of Abraham and Jesus loosed me from the bond of sickness.

Chapter 5 ~ Healing Confessions

Galatians 3:29
And if ye be Christ's, then are ye Abraham's seed, and heirs according to the promise.

Luke 13:12–13, 16
And when Jesus saw her, he called her to him, and said unto her, Woman, thou art loosed from thine infirmity. And he laid his hands on her: and immediately she was made straight, and glorified God.

And ought not this woman, being a daughter of Abraham, whom Satan hath bound, lo, these eighteen years, be loosed from this bond on the sabbath day?

Jesus bore my sicknesses and carried my pains.

Isaiah 53:4
Surely he hath borne our griefs, and carried our sorrows: yet we did esteem him stricken, smitten of God, and afflicted.

Jesus was wounded, bruised, and beaten to make me free from sin, sickness, and disease.

Isaiah 53:5
But he was wounded (tormented) for our transgressions, he was bruised for our iniquities: the chastisement of our peace was upon him; and with his stripes (bruises) we are healed.

I touch the hem of Jesus' garment through my prayer and faith, and I am healed and made whole.

Treasures in Heaven

Mark 5:25-34

And a certain woman, which had an issue of blood twelve years,

And had suffered many things of many physicians, and had spent all that she had, and was nothing bettered, but rather grew worse,

When she had heard of Jesus, came in the press behind, and touched his garment (25-27).

For she said, If I may touch but his clothes, I shall be whole (28).

And straightway the fountain of her blood was dried up; and she felt in her body that she was healed of that plague (29).

And Jesus, immediately knowing in himself that virtue had gone out of him, turned him about in the press, and said, Who touched my clothes (30)?

And his disciples said unto him, Thou seest the multitude thronging thee, and sayest thou, Who touched me (31)?

And he looked round about to see her that had done this thing (32).

But the woman fearing and trembling, knowing what was done in her, came and fell down before him, and told him all the truth (33).

And he said unto her, Daughter, thy faith hath made thee whole; go in peace, and be whole of thy plague (34).

Chapter 5 ~ Healing Confessions

The healing anointing of Jesus Christ is flowing from the top of my head to the soles of my feet as I speak these words of life.

Proverbs 18:21
Death and life are in the power of the tongue: and they that love it shall eat the fruit thereof.

I command sickness and disease to be removed from my body right now in the name of Jesus, and I receive full restoration in its place.

Mark 11:22-23
And Jesus answering saith unto them, Have faith in God (have the faith of God). For verily I say unto you, That whosoever shall say unto this mountain, Be thou removed, and be thou cast into the sea; and shall not doubt in his heart, but shall believe that those things which he saith shall come to pass; he shall have whatsoever he saith.

I have faith in the Word of God; therefore, nothing is impossible unto me.

Matthew 17:20
And Jesus said unto them, Because of your unbelief: for verily I say unto you, If ye have faith as a grain of mustard seed, ye shall say unto this mountain, Remove hence to yonder place; and it shall remove; and nothing shall be impossible unto you.

Jesus is moved with compassion on my behalf and His mercies never end.

Treasures in Heaven

Matthew 14:14
And Jesus went forth, and saw a great multitude, and was moved with compassion toward them, and he healed their sick.

Lamentations 3:21-23
But this I call to mind, and therefore I have hope: The steadfast love of the LORD never ceases, his mercies never come to an end; they are new every morning; great is thy faithfulness.

Psalm 23:6
Surely goodness and mercy shall follow me all the days of my life: and I will dwell in the house of the LORD for ever.

Jesus came unto me with abundant life and healing in his wings.

Malachi 4:2
But unto you that fear my name shall the Sun of righteousness arise with healing in his wings; and ye shall go forth, and grow up as calves of the stall.

John 10:10
The thief cometh not, but for to steal, and to kill, and to destroy: I am come that they might have life, and that they might have it more abundantly.

Jesus set me free from the works of the devil.

Chapter 5 ~ Healing Confessions

1 John 3:8b
For this purpose the Son of God was manifested, that he might destroy the works of the devil.

Acts 10:38
How God anointed Jesus of Nazareth with the Holy Ghost and with power: who went about doing good, and healing all that were oppressed of the devil; for God was with him.

I overcome everything that comes my way today, because God is with me and this is my year of new beginnings.

Jeremiah 30:17
For I will restore health unto thee, and I will heal thee of thy wounds, saith the LORD; because they called thee an Outcast, saying, This is Zion, whom no man seeketh after.

Romans 8:35-39
Who shall separate us from the love of Christ? shall tribulation, or distress, or persecution, or famine, or nakedness, or peril, or sword?

As it is written, For thy sake we are killed all the day long; we are accounted as sheep for the slaughter (35-36).

Nay, in all these things we are more than conquerors through him that loved us (37).

For I am persuaded, that neither death, nor life, nor angels, nor principalities, nor powers, nor things present, nor things to come,
Nor height, nor depth, nor any other creature, shall be able to separate us from the love of God, which is in Christ Jesus our Lord (38-39).

Treasures in Heaven

Jesus blessed me with healing and made me a blessing to others.

Psalm 67:2
That thy way may be known upon earth, thy saving health among all nations.

Thank you for these wonderful blessings, in Jesus mighty Name. Amen!

Treasure Chest

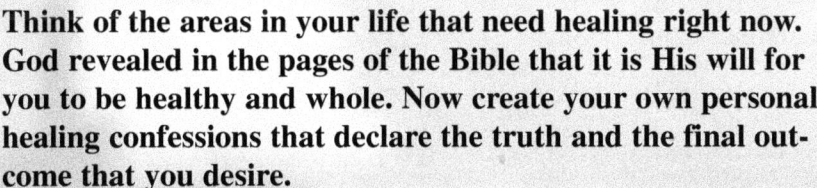

The prayer of faith shall save the sick. Faith comes by hearing the Word of God *over* and *over* again, because then you will know the truth and it will make you free. If you don't know that God wants you healthy, then you don't know the truth yet.

Think of the areas in your life that need healing right now. God revealed in the pages of the Bible that it is His will for you to be healthy and whole. Now create your own personal healing confessions that declare the truth and the final outcome that you desire.

Sickness:

Scripture References:

Personal Confession:

Sickness:

Scripture References:

Treasures in Heaven

Personal Confession:

Sickness:

Scripture References:

Personal Confession:

Section Three
Hidden Treasure

The Father's Gift to us in the person of Holy Spirit has been, for many years, treated as something to be hidden or forbidden. But neither should be the case. Holy Spirit is a gift that should be highly treasured and openly shared. A lack of knowledge in this area is what stops us from fully tapping into the wonderful treasures He has to offer.

Treasures in Heaven

Treasures in Heaven
Chapter Six

The Names of Holy Spirit

This section will help you get to know Holy Spirit in a personal and intimate way. I know Holy Spirit by His Names. He is the:

Spirit of Truth
John 16:13
Howbeit when he, the Spirit of truth, is come, he will guide you into all truth: for he shall not speak of himself; but whatsoever he shall hear, that shall he speak: and he will shew you things to come.

Spirit of Holiness
Romans 1:4
And declared to be the Son of God with power, according to the spirit of holiness, by the resurrection from the dead.

Spirit of Life
Romans 8:2
For the law of the Spirit of life in Christ Jesus

hath made me free from the law of sin and death.

Spirit of Adoption
Romans 8:15
For ye have not received the spirit of bondage again to fear; but ye have received the Spirit of adoption, whereby we cry, Abba, Father.

Spirit of Grace
Hebrews 10:29
Of how much sorer punishment, suppose ye, shall he be thought worthy, who hath trodden under foot the Son of God, and hath counted the blood of the covenant, wherewith he was sanctified, an unholy thing, and hath done despite unto the Spirit of grace?

Spirit of The Glory of God
1 Peter 4:14
If ye be reproached for the name of Christ, happy are ye; for the spirit of glory and of God resteth upon you: on their part he is evil spoken of, but on your part he is glorified.

Spirit of Love
Romans 15:30
Now I beseech you, brethren, for the Lord Jesus Christ's sake, and for the love of the Spirit, that ye strive together with me in your prayers to God for me.

Chapter 6 ~ The Names of Holy Spirit

Spirit of Promise
Ephesians 1:13
In whom ye also trusted, after that ye heard the word of truth, the gospel of your salvation: in whom also after that ye believed, ye were sealed with that Holy Spirit of promise.

Treasures in Heaven

Treasures in Heaven
Chapter Seven

The Emblems of Holy Spirit

When you know the emblems of God, the more you will be able to recognize how He is working in your everyday life. I know Holy Spirit by His emblems. He is:

A Dove Who brings order, peace, and comfort

Matthew 3:16
And Jesus, when he was baptized, went up straightway out of the water: and, lo, the heavens were opened unto him, and he saw the Spirit of God descending like a dove, and lighting upon him.

An Anointing Oil Who brings consecration, illumination, and joy

Treasures in Heaven

Anointed to overflow:

Psalm 23:5
Thou preparest a table before me in the presence of mine enemies: thou anointest my head with oil; my cup runneth over.

Anointed to service:

Acts 10:38
How God anointed Jesus of Nazareth with the Holy Ghost and with power: who went about doing good, and healing all that were oppressed of the devil; for God was with him.

Anointed to bring good news:

Luke 4:18,19
The Spirit of the Lord is upon me, because he hath anointed me to preach the gospel to the poor; he hath sent me to heal the brokenhearted, to preach deliverance to the captives, and recovering of sight to the blind, to set at liberty them that are bruised, To preach the acceptable year of the Lord.

Anointed to know the Lord:

1 John 2:18,20
Little children, it is the last time: and as ye have heard that antichrist shall come, even now are there many antichrists; whereby we know that it is the last time. But ye have an unction from the Holy One, and ye know all things.

Chapter 7 ~ The Emblems of Holy Spirit

A fire that brings purification, judgment, and vindication

Luke 3:16
John answered, saying unto them all, I indeed baptize you with water; but one mightier than I cometh, the latchet of whose shoes I am not worthy to unloose: he shall baptize you with the Holy Ghost and with fire.

Like Water that brings refreshing, fruitfulness, and evidence of abundant grace

A satisfied thirst:

John 4:14
But whosoever drinketh of the water that I shall give him shall never thirst; but the water that I shall give him shall be in him a well of water springing up into everlasting life. He brings a rain of restoration.

A Holy Environment Who brings a place for God's character to grow

A new place to walk:

Galatians 5:16, 22, 23
This I say then, Walk in the Spirit, and ye shall not fulfill the lust of the flesh. But the fruit of the Spirit is love, joy, peace, longsuffering, gentleness, goodness, faith, Meekness, temperance: against such there is no law.

A new way to live:

> **Romans 8:11,12,13**
> But if the Spirit of him that raised up Jesus from the dead dwell in you, he that raised up Christ from the dead shall also quicken your mortal bodies by his Spirit that dwelleth in you. Therefore, brethren, we are debtors, not to the flesh, to live after the flesh. For if ye live after the flesh, ye shall die: but if ye through the Spirit do mortify the deeds of the body, ye shall live.

A Wind Who brings life and power

> **John 20:22**
> And when he had said this, he breathed on them, and saith unto them, Receive ye the Holy Ghost.

Like Clothing Who brings equipping, endowment, and strength

> **Luke 24:49**
> And, behold, I send the promise of my Father upon you: but tarry ye in the city of Jerusalem, until ye be endued with power from on high.

An Earnest Who brings a taste of future glory

> **2 Corinthians 5:5**
> Now he that hath wrought us for the selfsame thing is God, who also hath given unto us the earnest of the Spirit.

Treasures in Heaven
Chapter Eight

The Power and Ability of Holy Spirit Abides in Me

The power and ability of Holy Spirit abides in me. He is my personal:

Teacher
1 John 2:20,27
But ye have an unction from the Holy One, and ye know all things. But the anointing which ye have received of him abideth in you, and ye need not that any man teach you: but as the same anointing teacheth you of all things, and is truth, and is no lie, and even as it hath taught you, ye shall abide in him.

Helper
Romans 8:26
Likewise the Spirit also helpeth our infirmities: for we know not what we should pray for as we ought: but the Spirit itself maketh intercession for us with groanings which cannot be uttered.

Advocate
1 John 2:1
My little children, these things write I unto you, that ye sin not. And if any man sin, we have an advocate with the Father, Jesus Christ the righteous.

Counselor
Colossians 3:15
And let the peace of God rule in your hearts, to the which also ye are called in one body; and be ye thankful.

Comforter
Ephesians 5:18,19
And be not drunk with wine, wherein is excess; but be filled with the Spirit; Speaking to yourselves in psalms and hymns and spiritual songs, singing and making melody in your heart to the Lord.

Intercessor
Romans 8:27
And he that searcheth the hearts knoweth what is the mind of the Spirit, because he maketh intercession for the saints according to the will of God.

Strengthener
James 4:5-7
Do ye think that the scripture saith in vain, The spirit that dwelleth in us lusteth to envy? But he giveth more grace. Wherefore he saith, God

Chapter 8 ~ The Power and Ability of Holy Spirit

resisteth the proud, but giveth grace unto the humble. Submit yourselves therefore to God. Resist the devil, and he will flee from you.

Standby
Hebrews 13:5b, 6
For he hath said, I will never leave thee, nor forsake thee. So that we may boldly say, The Lord is my helper, and I will not fear what man shall do unto me.

Treasure Chest

Jesus loves you so much! He wants you to be equipped to win in every area of life. Not only did He come to give us life and life more abundantly, then went back to the right hand of Father to continually make intercessions for us, but also He sent us a personal Guide and Comforter in the Person of Holy Spirit. (John 10:10; Hebrews 7:25; John 14:16; 16:13)

Knowing that the power and ability of Holy Spirit abides in you should cause you to be confident in any situation or circumstance. Always remember the magnitude of this *hidden treasure* within you, and be assured that you have personal access to everything you need. However, you must also remember to ask for help!

In the following examples I have shared some general areas with which Holy Spirit assists me. Jot down some general and/or specific areas that you may need His assistance.

As my Teacher: You teach me how to be a leader and how to submit to others. You teach me how to start a business. You teach me how to get wealth.

As my Helper: You help me to find the right job, mate, and home. You help me to grow up. You help me to carry out my assignment.

As my Advocate or Lawyer: You defend me when I am falsely accused. You represent me in matters too great for me.

As my Counselor: You give me wise counsel. You give me insight into the true nature of the people and things that try to enter my life.

As my Comforter: You lift me out of despair and depression. You heal my broken heart.

Treasures in Heaven

As my Intercessor: You pray the perfect will of the Father on my behalf when I don't know how.

As my Strengthener: When I am weak you exchange strengths with me to make me strong.

As my Standby: You always cover my back when others stand me up.

Treasures in Heaven
Chapter Nine

The Power and Ability of Holy Spirit Rest on Me

Not only do you have the power and ability of Holy Spirit abiding on the inside of you, but also you have His anointing resting upon you. The power and ability of Holy Spirit rests upon me. I have the:

Spirit of Wisdom
Insight to accomplish the will of God completely and to the smallest detail without turning to the right or the left

Spirit of Understanding
Knowledge of the Scriptures

Spirit of Counsel
Ability to share wisdom and knowledge at the right time and in the right way

Spirit of Might
Power and ability to perform miracles

Gifts of healing to minister to great multitudes

Spirit of Knowledge of God
Personal and intimate fellowship with the Father

Spirit of Fear of the Lord
Respect, awe, reverence, obedience, and sensitivity to the Father

Spirit of Delight in the Fear of the Lord
Quick discernment and intuitive knowledge in every situation

Isaiah 11:2-3
And the spirit of the LORD shall rest upon him, the spirit of wisdom and understanding, the spirit of counsel and might, the spirit of knowledge and of the fear of the LORD; And shall make him of quick understanding in the fear of the LORD: and he shall not judge after the sight of his eyes, neither reprove after the hearing of his ears.

Treasures in Heaven
Chapter Ten

Speaking in Tongues

People often wonder why they should be baptized with Holy Spirit with Bible evidence of speaking with other tongues. But there are many wonderful benefits that God designed for us to have as we tap into this Gift of Holy Spirit. There are ten reasons I speak in tongues. Speaking in tongues:

Is my initial, outward manifestation of Holy Spirit's baptism

Acts 2:1-4
And when the day of Pentecost was fully come, they were all with one accord in one place. And suddenly there came a sound from heaven as of a rushing mighty wind, and it filled all the house where they were sitting. And there appeared unto them cloven tongues like as of fire, and it sat upon each of them. And they were all filled with the Holy Ghost, and began to speak with other tongues, as the Spirit gave them utterance.

Treasures in Heaven

Provides me with spiritual edification
Jude 20
But ye, beloved, building up yourselves on your most holy faith, praying in the Holy Ghost.

Reminds me of Holy Spirit's indwelling presence.
John 14:16,17
And I will pray the Father, and he shall give you another Comforter, that he may abide with you for ever; Even the Spirit of truth; whom the world cannot receive, because it seeth him not, neither knoweth him: but ye know him; for he dwelleth with you, and shall be in you.

Keeps my prayers in line with God's will.
Romans 8:26,27
Likewise the Spirit also helpeth our infirmities: for we know not what we should pray for as we ought: but the Spirit itself maketh intercession for us with groanings which cannot be uttered. And he that searcheth the hearts knoweth what is the mind of the Spirit, because he maketh intercession for the saints according to the will of God.

Praying in tongues helps me to pray when I don't know how. When I pray in tongues, Holy Spirit searches the intents and motives of the soul and spirit, and applies perfect wisdom to the real need.

Stimulates my faith

Chapter 10 ~ Speaking in Tongues

Jude 20,21
But ye, beloved, building up yourselves on your most holy faith, praying in the Holy Ghost, Keep yourselves in the love of God, looking for the mercy of our Lord Jesus Christ unto eternal life.

I stimulate my faith by watering and nourishing the Word I already have in me and by keeping myself in God's love; Faith works by love.

Keeps me free from worldly contamination

James 1:27b
And to keep himself unspotted from the world.

Allows me to speak forth the mysteries of Christ

1 Corinthians 14:2
For he that speaketh in an unknown tongue speaketh not unto men, but unto God: for no man understandeth him; howbeit in the spirit he speaketh mysteries.

As I speak in tongues, revelation about my inheritance comes to my spirit, enlightens my mind, and provides me with edification. I am speaking directly from my spirit to my Father's Spirit.

Gives me spiritual refreshing

Isaiah 28:11,12
For with stammering lips and another tongue will he speak to this people. To whom he said, This

is the rest wherewith ye may cause the weary to rest; and this is the refreshing.

Is giving thanks unto Him
1 Corinthians 14:14,17
For if I pray in an unknown tongue, my spirit prayeth, but my understanding is unfruitful. For thou verily givest thanks well, but the other is not edified.

Brings my tongue under subjection
James 3:8
But the tongue can no man tame; it is an unruly evil, full of deadly poison.

No natural ability can tame the tongue. When I yield my tongue to God by my prayer language, He can bring forth blessings and right words that edify.

Treasures in Heaven
Chapter Eleven

The Holy Spirit Baptism
*How to Receive the Baptism
of the Holy Ghost*

Now that you know about this wonderful Gentleman by the name of Holy Spirit, the Third Person of the Trinity, you can enable Him to abide with you and within you forever!

We serve a God who likes to give great gifts: Salvation is His gift to the world; and Holy Spirit is a gift He desires to give to His very own kids, those who have already received His son, Jesus Christ! The Word of God says that Holy Spirit is the Promise, Comforter, Gift, and the Power.

He is the Promise

Luke 24:49
And, behold, I send the promise of my Father upon you: but tarry ye in the city of Jerusalem, until ye be endued with power from on high.

Luke 11:9-13
And I say unto you, Ask, and it shall be given

you; seek, and ye shall find; knock, and it shall be opened unto you (9).

For every one that asketh receiveth; and he that seeketh findeth; and to him that knocketh it shall be opened (10).

If a son shall ask bread of any of you that is a father, will he give him a stone? Or if he ask a fish, will he for a fish give him a serpent (11-12)?

If ye then, being evil, know how to give good gifts unto your children: how much more shall your heavenly Father give the Holy Spirit to them that ask him (13)?

He is the Comforter

John 14:16, 17, 26
And I will pray the Father, and he shall give you another Comforter, that he may abide with you forever;

Even the Spirit of Truth; whom the world cannot receive, because it seeth Him not, neither knoweth Him: but ye know Him; for he dwelleth with you, and shall be in you (16-17).

But the Comforter, which is the Holy Ghost, whom the Father will send in my name, He shall teach you all things, and bring all things to your remembrance, whatsoever I have said unto you (26).

Chapter 11 ~ The Holy Spirit Baptism

This is Jesus speaking, letting us know that the Holy Spirit is from God. As you can see, Jesus didn't want to leave us comfortless and without power or direction. This word "comforter" is from the Greek word "paraclete," and it means: Helper, Standby, Teacher, Counselor, Strengthener, Advocate, and Intercessor. (I told you God gives good gifts!) When we receive Holy Spirit, we can enjoy all the benefits of His personality and these attributes.

He is a Gift

Acts 2:38
Then Peter said unto them, Repent and be baptized every one of you in the name of Jesus Christ for the remission of sins, and ye shall receive the gift of the Holy Ghost.

This is the easiest thing you have ever done! Why do I say that? Because all you have to do is ask and receive Him! In other words, you don't have to beg for Him, work for Him, usher for Him, or sing in the choir for Him. Just reach out and receive the gift of the Holy Spirit. Amen! God gives, you receive. Say, "God gives and I receive." Most of the time, gifts come in wrapping paper or in a box, but all you have to do is unwrap and enjoy!

He Gives You Power

Acts 1:8
But ye shall receive power, after that the Holy Ghost is come upon you: and ye shall be witnesses unto me both in Jerusalem, and in all Judea, and in Samaria, and unto the uttermost part of the earth.

The word "power" here is translated "dunamis," and it means dynamite, explosive ability. You're going to be a dynamic witness for Jesus, because you're infused with His power to impact lives when you receive His gift of Holy Spirit.

How Do You Know What You Are Saying?

I Corinthians 14:2
For he that speaketh in an unknown tongue speaketh not unto men, but unto God: for no man understandeth him; howbeit in the spirit he speaketh mysteries.

This means you are actually talking directly to God, you are speaking mysteries, and you are praising and magnifying God, offering perfect praise from your spirit to His Spirit.

The Bible Evidence of Speaking In Tongues

Acts 2:1-4
And when the day of Pentecost was fully come, they were all with one accord in one place.

And suddenly there came a sound from heaven as of a rushing mighty wind, and it filled all the house where they were sitting (1-2).

And there appeared unto them cloven tongues like as of fire, and it sat upon each of them (3).

And they were all filled with the Holy Ghost, and began to speak with other tongues, as the Spirit gave them utterance (4).

Chapter 11 ~ The Holy Spirit Baptism

Let's pay close attention to the details in verse four, because it tells us how to open or unwrap your gift. *First*, it says, they were all filled with the Holy Ghost. Notice how many were filled. *Second*, it says they began to speak with other tongues. Who did the speaking? They did. You open your gift by opening your mouth to speak! So first you are filled and then you speak; or first you receive the gift, then you unwrap it! Think about the last time you received a gift, you probably didn't open it timidly, but instead, you boldly tore open that package! That's what you're going to do today!

Third, it says they spoke as the Spirit gave them utterance. In other words, the Spirit gave the enunciation. He will give you the style or manner of speech, but He will not make you speak. Remember, I told you that He is a Gentleman. It's not all you, and it's not all Holy Spirit, but it is a joint effort between you both. You get the easy part. Just open your mouth and use your voice!

How Do You Know You're Filled

Acts 10:44-46
While Peter yet spake these words, the Holy Ghost fell on all them which heard the word.

And they of the circumcision which believed were astonished, as many as came with Peter, because that on the Gentiles also was poured out the gift of the Holy Ghost (44-45).

For they heard them speak with tongues, and magnify God (46).

Treasures in Heaven

The way you will know that you have received your Gift is simply because you received it by faith in the Word of God. The way someone else will know that you received your gift is because they will be able to hear you speak with other tongues. You can begin to enjoy this powerful and priceless treasure today.

Remember that we said it is not all you and it is not all Holy Spirit. It is a joint effort between you and the Spirit of God. You supply your faith, will, and your voice box, and He will supply the manner or style by which you speak. Now stand to your feet and pray this prayer out loud:

> Father, your Word says that the Holy Spirit is a gift. He is a gift. I don't work for Him; all I do is receive Him. So Father, I receive, right now, as an act of my will and my faith, the Holy Spirit, with the Bible Evidence of Speaking with other tongues. I will not be embarrassed. I will not shake my head no! But I will speak with other tongues on the count of three.

All right, let's count: 1-2-3. Take a deep breath, and now speak in other tongues. This is not praying in English, but it might sound like baby talk or gibberish. That's okay. Don't worry about the way it sounds. Just say it and get it out of your mouth. As you use your new prayer language everyday, you will become more fluent.

Treasure Chest

Do you trust someone that you don't know? Not usually. It is only after we get to know something about that person's character and what they are all about that we will begin to trust and rely on them. We must get to know Holy Spirit intimately so that we can call upon Him with total confidence and know that He will help us in our weaknesses and inabilities.

Think of current situations in your life right now that can benefit from the help of Holy Spirit. What attributes and abilities of Holy Spirit will cause you to be victorious in that situation? Now create your own personal confessions and/or prayers that declare your trust and reliance upon His character and power to bring about necessary change.

Situation:

Holy Spirit's name, emblem, or function:

Personal Confession:

Treasures in Heaven

Situation:

Holy Spirit's name, emblem, or function:

Personal Confession:

Section Four
Power-Packed Prayers

The Word of God is powerful and sharper than a two-edged sword. Therefore, when you pack your prayers with the Word, you are packing tremendous power! Praying according to what God has already declared in His Word shows your confidence in Him.

Also, as you pray the prayer of spiritual growth for yourself and for your loved ones, you will not only begin to see increase in your spiritual life, but also in their spiritual lives.

Treasures in Heaven

Treasures in Heaven
Chapter Twelve

Model Prayers

Model Prayer for Your Pastor

Dear Heavenly Father, I come before you in the name of Jesus, thanking you and praising you for raising up my pastor and our first family for this hour. I ask that you continue to guard and protect them from all hurt, harm, and danger along their daily walk and in all their travels. I speak great grace and peace into every area of their lives—nothing missing, broken, or torn, but everything whole. I declare divine health and healing in their bodies, right now, even as I speak. I also declare unity within their family. Teach them how to flow with one another and encourage one another at all times and under every circumstance.

Father, please give my pastor wisdom in every situation, circumstance, and decisions that he makes. I thank you that he or she operates with utmost integrity in all that he says and does. My pastor will not miss it to the right nor to the left, but will continue to choose the right people, locations, buildings, and

Treasures in Heaven

will have the right timing in everything. I thank you for providing all the necessary resources, whether it is human resources, natural resources, or financial resources. Thank you for granting unto my pastor favor with all government officials, courts, and dignitaries. Open doors for my pastor that cannot be shut. Deliver my pastor from unreasonable, ungodly men, and surround my pastor with faithful men and women at all times.

I pray that my pastor's heart stays soft before You and that he or she remains meek and humble in all fear and trembling. Help my pastor to create a productive, yet stress-free work environment, anointing my pastor and all our employees with the oil of joy and gladness, while giving them sweatless victory in every project and endeavor. I speak unity and peace among every staff member, and I bind any strife or discord. Let each minister esteem the other as better than themselves honoring, preferring, and loving one another.

Allow the Gifts of the Spirit to operate in our ministry mightily. Increase the anointing on my pastor's life on down to every member, and cause us all to abound in love toward all men. I pray that my pastor continues to proclaim and rightly divide the full counsel of the Word of Truth, speaking boldly as he or she ought to speak with all patience and longsuffering.

Father, when my pastor's heart is overwhelmed, lead him or her to the Rock of Refreshing, in Jesus Name. Amen!

Chapter 12 ~ Model Prayers

Model Prayer for Mate
The Prayer of Her Heart

Dear Heavenly Father, I come before you in the name of Jesus, thanking You and praising You for my mate. Thank You for raising him up for this hour, and for keeping him under your wing. Thank you for surrounding him with Your mighty love and protection and strengthening his inner-man, causing him to be strong in spirit, soul and body. Let Your peace rule and reign in his heart and mind, even right now as I speak.

> **Proverbs 31:23**
> Her husband is known in the gates, when he sitteth among the elders of the land.

Continue to soften and melt his heart before You while ministering to all the secret places of his heart. Pull on his every heartstring and turn his every desire toward You. Lord, I thank You that he is sensitive to your Spirit, familiar with your voice, and obedient to your Word. Let him increasingly see Your Glory, taste of Your Goodness, and be changed by Your righteous judgments. Reveal to him Your master plan and timing and his part in it. Show him great and mighty things, which he has not yet known.

Teach him Your Ways and Your very Heart. Teach his hands to war, and his fingers to fight against wrong thoughts, bad habits, and temptations of any kind. Help him to recognize and renounce anything that tries to exalt itself against You and Your Word. Deliver him from every evil work. Restore, refresh, and renew his soul. Lord, daily purify and sanctify him, and use him as a vessel unto righteousness.

Treasures in Heaven

Father, because of You, he is a man of integrity and honor. He walks uprightly before You and before all men. He is a faithful server and a cheerful giver. His delight is in Your Word and in Your very presence. He is a man of prayer. His character and good name precedes him. He is blameless, vigilant, sober, of good behavior, given to hospitality, apt to teach, not given to wine, not greedy of filthy lucre; but patient, not a brawler, not covetous, but is nourished up in the words of faith and of good doctrine.

He is a strong man, meek and humbly submitted to godly and natural authority. He is a prosperous man not lacking anything. His desire is to see souls saved, lives changed, people delivered and set free. He is ever ready and willing to minister the gospel in word and deed. He is quick to repent, and quick to forgive. *Father he is a man after your own heart; he is my mate.*

Chapter 12 ~ Model Prayers

Model Prayer for Mate
The Prayer of His Heart

Dear Heavenly Father, I give You heartfelt praise and earnest thanks for my mate whom You have chosen and prepared for me since the beginning of time. She was raised in Your fear and admonition, but she still comes boldly with her petitions to Your throne of grace. She is also bold to bear witness as a true ambassador of Your kingdom, being ever ready to tell of Your goodness, mercy and grace. She has a conscious faith and is keenly aware of Your Life that flows within her as the vine that flows into its branches.

She is obedient to Your statutes and is willing to accept the assignment You have for her life, and she is diligent in all her workings to see its fulfillment. In her mountaintop experiences she remains humble by worshiping You in reverent praise. Even in her valleys, she blesses Your Holy Name. Reveal to her Your vision and purpose for her life that she may see herself more through Your eyes than through her own. Daily sanctify and wash her by the truth of Your Word that nothing unlike You may be found in her.

Cause Your indwelling Spirit to quicken and illuminate her and to transform her more into Your express image which will enable her to easily find forgiveness for anyone who trespasses against her. Let Your Spirit also inspire her to quick and earnest repentance when she does miss the mark. Break up any fallow ground in her heart that may hinder her walk, that she be not led into any temptation. Continue to be a lamp unto her feet and a light unto her path that she may avoid the traps and snares of the evil one, for my mate is free from her past.

She is not emotionally confined or mentally imprisoned, as she knows no limitations in You.

Father, glorify Your Name through her words, her deeds, and her very life. Allow Your glory to manifest in her that all who may see will marvel at Your wondrous works. As the brightness of Your glory is risen upon her, her life will shine as a reflection in the mirror of Your will. Whatever she sets her hand to do will prosper because of her intimacy with You. Every seed that she plants will produce quick and bountiful harvests. She girds herself with strength, opens her mouth with wisdom, and on her tongue is the law of kindness. Her own works praise her in the gates.

She is tender, loving, compassionate, and sincere in all her dealings. She is attentive, humble, of good character, generous, faithful, and of a nurturing spirit. She is a true Proverbs 31 woman, a virtuous wife!

Lastly, I also pray that You knit our hearts together that we may be tuned in to the key of Your Spirit, perfecting us in love. In that agreement, anything that we ask, we know will be granted.

Father, I thank You that You have heard me! In Jesus' Name I pray. Amen.

Chapter 12 ~ Model Prayers

Bible Prayers for Spiritual Growth

This I pray, that my love may abound yet more and more in knowledge and in all judgment; that I may approve things that are excellent; that I may be sincere and without offence till the day of Christ; being filled with the fruits of righteousness, which are by Jesus Christ, unto the glory and praise of God (Philippians 1:9-11).

For this cause I also do not cease to pray, and to desire that I might be filled with the knowledge of his will in all wisdom and spiritual understanding; That I might walk worthy of the Lord unto all pleasing, being fruitful in every good work, and increasing in the knowledge of God; Strengthened with all might, according to his glorious power, unto all patience and longsuffering with joyfulness; Giving thanks unto the Father, which hath made me able to be a partaker of the inheritance of the saints in light: Who hath delivered us from the power of darkness, and hath translated us into the kingdom of his dear Son (Colossians 1:9-13).

That the God of our Lord Jesus Christ, the Father of glory, may give unto me the spirit of wisdom and revelation in the knowledge of him: The eyes of my understanding being enlightened; that I may know what is the hope of his calling, and what the riches of the glory of his inheritance in the saints, And what is the exceeding greatness of his power to us-ward who believe, according to the working of his mighty power, Which he wrought in Christ, when he raised him from the dead, and set him at his own right hand in the heavenly places, Far above all principality, and power, and might, and dominion, and every name that is named, not only in this world, but also in that which is to come (Ephesians 1:17-21).

Treasures in Heaven

For this cause I bow my knees unto the Father of our Lord Jesus Christ, Of whom the whole family in heaven and earth is named, That he would grant me, according to the riches of his glory, to be strengthened with might by his Spirit in my inner man; That Christ may dwell in my heart by faith; that I, being rooted and grounded in love, May be able to comprehend with all saints what is the breadth, and length, and depth, and height; And to know the love of Christ, which passeth knowledge, that I might be filled with all the fullness of God. Now unto him that is able to do exceeding abundantly above all that I ask or think, according to the power that worketh in me (Ephesians 3:14-20). In Jesus' Name, Amen.

Treasure Chest

Did you know that the Bible tells us that we are to pray for all men; for kings, and for all those that are in authority in order that we can lead a quiet and peaceable life in all godliness and honesty? (I Timothy 2:2)

Think of those persons in your life right now that are in authority. Our president, pastor, supervisor, teachers are all good examples of who God wants us to pray for. Now create your own personal prayers that declare the final outcome that you desire.

Leaders:

Scripture References:

Personal Prayer:

Treasures in Heaven

Leaders:

Scripture References:

Personal Prayer:

Others:

Scripture References:

Personal Prayer:

Treasures in Heaven

Personal Prayer for Mate:

Treasures in Heaven

Section Five
Divine Declarations

These are Scriptures that declare God's promise to take care of us no matter what is going on. In the end, we win. We know and believe this whether or not we actually see any evidence of victory. But soon, every knee shall bow and every tongue will confess that Jesus is Lord of Heaven and Earth!

Treasures in Heaven

Treasures in Heaven
Chapter Thirteen

There Shall Be Righteousness In The Land

Truly the days are evil because people have no regard for God or man. This generation exalts evil and takes pleasure in wickedness and deceit. Some actually hate truth and goodness, and others think it's just unattainable. But God will cause righteousness and praise to spring forth before all men. So its time for us to take Him at His word and arise and shine for the glory of the Lord is risen upon us.

2 Timothy 3:13, 14
But evil men and seducers shall wax worse and worse, deceiving, and being deceived. But continue thou in the things, which thou hast learned and hast been assured of, knowing of whom thou hast learned them.

Isaiah 59:19
So shall they fear the name of the Lord from the west, and his glory from the rising of the sun. When the enemy shall come in like a flood, the Spirit of the Lord shall lift up a standard against him.

I John 4:4
Ye are of God, little children, and have overcome them: because greater is he that is in you, than he that is in the world.

Psalm 46:10,11
Be still, and know that I am God: I will be exalted among the heathen; I will be exalted in the earth. The Lord of hosts is with us; the God of Jacob is our refuge. Selah.

Isaiah 45:8
Drop down ye heavens, from above, and let the skies pour down righteousness: let the earth open, and let them bring forth salvation, and let righteousness spring up together; I the Lord have created it.

Isaiah 61:11
For as the earth bringeth forth her bud, and as the garden causeth the things that are sown in it to spring forth; so the Lord God will cause righteousness and praise to spring forth before all the nations.

Isaiah 62:1,2a
For Zion's sake will I not hold my peace, and for Jerusalem's sake I will not rest, until the righteousness thereof go forth as brightness, and the salvation thereof as a lamp that burneth. And the Gentiles shall see thy righteousness, and all kings thy glory:

Isaiah 60:1-3
Arise, shine; for thy light is come, and the glory of the Lord is risen upon thee. For, behold, the

Chapter 13 ~ There Shall Be Righteousness in the Land

darkness shall cover the earth, and gross darkness the people: but the Lord shall arise upon thee, and his glory shall be seen upon thee.

And the Gentiles shall come to thy light, and kings to the brightness of thy rising.

Psalm 72:6,7
He shall come down like rain upon the mown grass: as showers that water the earth. In his days shall the righteous flourish; and abundance of peace so long as the moon endureth.

Joel 2:17-19,21
Let the priests, the ministers of the Lord, weep between the porch and the altar, and let them say, Spare thy people, O Lord, and give not thine heritage to reproach, that the heathen should rule over them: wherefore should they say among the people, Where is their God?

Then will the Lord be jealous for his land, and pity his people. Yea, the Lord will answer and say unto his people, Behold, I will send you corn, and wine, and oil, and ye shall be satisfied therewith: and I will no more make you a reproach among the heathen:

Fear not, O land; be glad and rejoice; for I the Lord will do great things.

Ezekiel 34:26
And I will make them and the places round about my hill a blessing; and I will cause the shower to come down in his season; there shall be showers of blessing.

Treasures in Heaven

Hosea 10:12
Sow to yourselves in righteousness, reap in mercy; break up your fallow ground: for it is time to seek the Lord, till he come and rain righteousness upon you.

Hosea 6:3
Then shall we know, if we follow on to know the Lord; his going forth is prepared as the morning; and he shall come unto us as the rain, as the latter and former rain unto the earth.

Zechariah 10:1
Ask ye of the Lord rain in the time of the latter rain; so the Lord shall make bright clouds, and give them showers of rain, to every one grass in the field.

Joel 2:23, 27, 28
Be glad then, ye children of Zion, and rejoice in the Lord your God: for he hath given you the former rain moderately, and he will cause to come down for you the rain, the former rain, and the latter rain in the first month.

And ye shall know that I am in the midst of Israel and that I am the Lord your God, and none else: and my people shall never be ashamed. And it shall come to pass afterward, that I will pour out my spirit upon all flesh.

Matthew 5:6; Isaiah 43:21
Blessed are they which do hunger and thirst after righteousness; for they shall be filled.

This people have I formed for myself; they shall shew forth my praise.

Chapter 13 ~ There Shall Be Righteousness in the Land

No matter what you see happening right now, never give up hope. Every one of these Scriptures must come to pass. But as you continue to believe and confess these promises, always remember the very heart and purpose of God.

2 Peter 3:9
The Lord is not slack concerning his promise, as some men count slackness; but is longsuffering to us-ward, not willing that any should perish, but that all should come to repentance.

Treasures in Heaven

Model Prayer for Righteousness in the Land

Dear Heavenly Father, I come boldly before you in the name of Jesus Christ of Nazareth. Father, You said in Your Word that when the enemy came in like a flood, you would raise up a standard against him. Therefore, I thank you for raising up that standard of righteousness against the evil of this day. No weapon formed against us shall prosper. We force back the spirit of antichrist with the mighty weapons of our warfare in all prayer and supplication.

Your Holy Spirit on the inside of us is greater than the spirit of antichrist in this world today. We overcome this present evil by the blood of the Lamb and the Word of our testimony. Since we reign with you in heavenly places, we use our authority and dominion right now by declaring that there shall be righteousness in this land. You will surely be exalted among the heathen. We loose the angels of God to go forth as flames of fire in the earth as a mighty hedge of protection around us, keeping us in all our ways.

Father, we thank you that the righteous are in authority and they shall flourish. Give our President uncommon wisdom and strength. Influence the Senate, Cabinet, CIA, FBI, Mayor, and every Government Official with the fear of the Lord. They will have an overwhelming desire to do the right thing in the eyes of God. Let the Judges of the land make righteous judgments. Turn the hearts of lawyers to be representatives of justice for all men and women. Shut the mouths of the liars. We bind up those lying spirits. We declare that the money-makers who are using their influence for evil will suddenly lose their riches. We command their wealth to be transferred into the hands of the righteous, right now, in the name of Jesus.

Chapter 13 ~ There Shall Be Righteousness in the Land

Father, give us supernatural wisdom and insight as we go to the polls and vote. Help us to discern the hearts of the candidates so that we can take a stand for what is right. Show us your plan in the earth, and our part in it. Give us this day our daily bread and our daily assignment. We set ourselves apart for You and your service so that your will may be done on earth as it is in heaven, In the Mighty name of Jesus. Amen.

God's Plan for Salvation

Let's begin by finding out where the **need** for salvation originated.

> **Romans 5:12**
> Wherefore, as by one man sin entered into the world, and death by sin; and so death passed upon all men, for that all have sinned.

As you can see, sin entered into the world through Adam, and so everyone born after Adam is a sinner, not just because they wanted to be one, but also because they inherited that sin nature. Of course, this was a problem. However God, in all His goodness, didn't leave us there. He provided the Solution.

> **John 3:16**
> For God so loved the world, that he gave his only begotten Son, that whosoever believeth in him should not perish, but have everlasting life.

For God so loved (**insert your name**) that He sent his Son. If you were the only person here on earth, God, the Father, still would have sent his Son to die for you.

Now let's look at the **Name** of this solution in the book of Acts.

> **Acts 4:10,12.**
> Be it known unto you all, and to all the people of Israel, that by the name of Jesus Christ of Nazareth, whom ye crucified, whom God raised from the dead, even by him doth this man stand here before you whole. Neither is there

Chapter 13 ~ There Shall Be Righteousness in the Land

salvation in any other: for there is none other name under heaven given among men, whereby we must be saved.

It's by the name of Jesus. Salvation is not found in any other name—not Mohammed, Buddha, or Hare Krishna. Only Jesus paid the price for men to be saved.

The solution is not automatic, because it needs to be **applied** to each person individually. This is how you apply the solution.

> **Romans 10:8-10**
> But what saith it? The word is nigh thee, even in thy mouth, and in thy heart: that is, the word of faith, which we preach; That if thou shalt confess with thy mouth the Lord Jesus, and shalt believe in thine heart that God hath raised him from the dead, thou shalt be saved. For with the heart man believeth unto righteousness; and with the mouth confession is made unto salvation.

The Bible says that if you believe in your heart, your inward being, that God raised Jesus from the dead, and then speak that belief out of your mouth, which seals it, you will be saved. It sounds really easy, doesn't it? It is. I'll show you in this next Scripture that God does indeed want it to be just that easy.

> **Ephesians 2:8, 9**
> For by grace are ye saved through faith; and that not of yourselves: it is the gift of God: Not of works, lest any man should boast.

This is something you can't work for, because it is a Gift. You just receive it. If you worked for it, it would no longer be a gift,

Treasures in Heaven

but a debt or payment that God owed to you. When God freely offers you a gift, then you have a **right to receive** it.

> **John 1:12**
> But as many as received him, to them gave he power to become the sons of God, even to them that believe on his name.

When you receive Jesus Christ as your personal Lord and Savior, he gives you the power and the authority to become a son of God!

If you have not yet received salvation according to the Word of God, please don't wait another minute. Pray the following prayer of salvation out loud.

> Dear Jesus, I believe in my heart that you died for me on the cross and that you arose on the third day. I confess to you that I am a sinner and that I need your love and forgiveness. Come into my life now, forgive my sins, and give me the free gift of eternal life. I confess you right now as my personal Lord and Savior. Thank you for paying the price for my salvation. Amen.

About The Author

Katherine E. Gardner is a graduate of Word of Faith Bible Training Center, 2000 (two-year diploma) and an active member of ten years at Word of Faith International Christian Center (WOFICC). WOFICC is located in Southfield, Michigan. Bishop Keith A. Butler is founder and pastor of WOFICC.

Katherine received Jesus Christ as her personal Lord and Savior in 1992 while attending Northwood University in Midland, Michigan. She also received her BBA in Marketing and Management in 1994. During that time, Katherine was elected to *Who's Who Among Students In American Universities & Colleges*.

As a student, Katherine conducted several formal speaking engagements and affected many lives for Christ. Because of her uncompromising and unashamed Christian lifestyle and the affect it had on campus and within the community, Katherine received the *Lavia A. Papini Humanitarian Award* from the faculty in the Graduation Honors Ceremony.

It is an honor and a privilege to witness the power of the Word of God as it transforms and changes the course of many lives.

For further information, please write:
Katherine E. Gardner
P.O. Box 530946
Livonia, MI 48153-0946

Treasures in Heaven

www.ingramcontent.com/pod-product-compliance
Lightning Source LLC
Chambersburg PA
CBHW060834050426
42453CB00008B/690